HOW TO FIND THE RIGHT WOMAN

D1407371

Broderick Boyd

CONTENTS

*"We were given the gift of life; it is up to us to give
ourselves the gift of living well."*
-Voltaire

BRODERICK BOYD

I magine walking onto a gorgeous sandy beach with your ideal woman with you. The warm breeze brushes your skin, and you can hear the soothing sound of the waves and the laugh of your beautiful, loving woman with you, loving you fully for the man you really are.

You both feel so connected mentally, physically, emotionally, sexually, and spiritually, and you feel totally confident, powerful, content and utterly happy, and fulfilled in your life, like you finally arrived where you really want to be…

Hi there! My name is Broderick Boyd, and for us to go deeper on this journey together, I'd like to begin with sharing a little bit more with you about my own journey to love and happiness and, hopefully, inspire you and show you what's now possible for you in your journey as well.

First off, I am SO grateful for this amazing life that I've created.

As I'm writing this book, I'm living here in the amazing Bay Area of California with my beautiful, loving, and supportive wife, Antia. Together, we both get to travel to beautiful locations, such as Hawaii, San Diego, Oregon, Disneyland, and really enjoy life fully together, living the life that we both always wanted to live.

And the thing I love so much about this relationship that I have now, is that I feel like I finally found a woman who really gets me fully, and I really get her. She loves me for who I really am, and I love her for who she really is. We also fully support each other on all levels, mentally, physically, emotionally, and spiritually.

I also love that we support and help each other through the tough times and the great times, enjoying life and also helping to change the world together, feeling totally fulfilled, content, confident, happy, and satisfied with the life and amazing relationship that we've been able to create.

And of course, it wasn't always like this for me.

My story begins growing up in a household where I felt very controlled by my mother, which is what I feel got me onto this path, originally.

Growing up, I felt like she was always telling me what I could do and what I couldn't do, and she was very overprotective of me. And she would keep me locked up in this little golden cage, where I was very comfortable and safe, but felt totally restricted and unhappy, and so I was pretty frustrated and angry about that growing up.

So, in those early stages, I felt that my heart closed off towards women and people, and I never wanted to be controlled by anyone (especially a woman) ever again.

Fast forward a few years, and I worked on breaking free of my parents' influence, and I got into college.

In college, I did a little work on myself. I read a couple of books, and pretty soon, I got into my first serious relationship.

This woman and I were together for about two-and-a-half years. And it was an OK relationship; we had our ups and downs. But after two and a half years of being together, she actually decided to dump me and to leave me.

And when she left me, I was actually very devastated by that.

I felt like I screwed it up, and I wasn't being the best man I could be. I felt guilty and sad for having it go the way it did.

It had gotten so low, at one point, I tried proposing to her after she broke up with me, and she said no, that she couldn't. We both cried, and I was just devastated.

I had worked on opening up my heart as much as I could during the relationship, but it just wasn't enough, and I was crushed.

So a few months after we broke up, I entered the deepest depression of my life.

I felt totally rejected, sad, alone, angry, and I had no great social life or social skills to turn to, and my confidence and my self-esteem was just shot and gone. This deep depression went on for about a year and a half.

And I remember, one day, I was sitting in my car in the depths of my depression, and I remember feeling this gaping black hole in my chest, just bleeding out.

And in that moment, I felt like this just wasn't working, and I should probably just end this. I actually considered killing myself and being done with it all.

Fortunately, however, in that moment I had thought about killing myself, a stronger, wiser, and more mature part of me came to my rescue, and that part said in that moment: "Sure Brody, you could kill yourself, but what if instead, as a fun experiment, you did WHATEVER IT TOOK to NEVER EVER EVER have to feel this way EVER again?"

And that's what I did.

So, I began my journey of studying EVERYTHING I can could get my hands on in the areas of women, dating, and building great confidence and social skills, without fear, and being the best man I could possible be.

I read hundreds of books on the subject, trying to master this.

I became so passionate that I also switched my college studies from Biology to Communication and Interpersonal Relationships and got my degree in that, because I was so passionate about mastering this area, and I wanted to learn as much about it as I could.

I also went to different workshops, seminars, and bootcamps to master this and figure out how to communicate with women and how to be great in relationships.

I went through the pickup artist community. I studied psychology and personal development, and I actually spent over $10,000 of my own money on different workshops, trainings, and courses, a lot which I put onto credit cards, because I had no money, but I was so committed to getting those new results in my life, and the alternative for me was death and misery.

And the frustrating thing was, after going through all this training and learning all of that information, I *still* wasn't able to connect with the high-quality woman that I really wanted to be with.

And that's when I finally said, "Okay, you know what? I'm going to find a man who's a true master of this, who's got this figured out." And I found a man that I resonated with, and I hired him as my coach.

He then took me under his wing and taught me all the things I needed to know, and he pointed out to me what I was doing right, what I was doing wrong, and what I need to be doing differently. He walked me through the path and held me accountable to taking the action towards that vision of what I wanted to create.

Shortly after that, I finally had the great breakthroughs and results I was looking for.

Then, I went through a phase where I was with dozens and dozens and dozens of very beautiful and amazing women, and I learned a lot about myself and about women in that phase.

But I soon realized that what I really wanted was to find a super high-quality woman to have a loving, long-term, and supportive relationship with, where we were both on the same page, supporting each other on all levels and working together to change the world and have a bigger purpose on the planet.

Shortly after I made that decision and while still working with my coach, I attracted my amazing, beautiful and loving wife, Antia, and life has been so amazing, fulfilling and magical…

So through that entire journey, THAT'S why I became so passionate about wanting to help other single men to build their confidence and social skills and find the right woman for them to share their life with and be happier, without loneliness, fear, or wasting any more time, and to not have to go through all of the dark struggles, and the trials and tribulations I had to go through.

At this point, I've helped thousands of men all over the world to start finding the right woman for them to share their life with and be happier for over 13+ years, and that's also why I created this amazing book, to help YOU to get jump-started in your journey to finding the lasting amazing love you've always wanted to have!

I've designed this book to be an ignition to your rocket ship, and the kick-in-the-pants that's going to take you into orbit to having an amazing life of your dreams, an amazing woman of your dreams, and to become the best man you can be, who's much more confident, without struggling with poor social skills, shyness, lack of confidence, rejection, anxiety, or putting in a lot of effort and not having it work out.

So as you go through this book, I recommended taking lots of notes, underlining passages that are valuable for you, and taking ACTION on what you learn.

Action is the only way that learning happens. You only learn something new when your behavior changes; otherwise, it's just information, and it will just be another book you read, and it will just be more data.

We want to turn that information into ACTION, and the way to do that is to look for specific action recommendations, even if it's just putting something on your to-do list or on your calendar to take action and DO THAT THING ASAP. It will be much more likely that you implement it and start to change and upgrade your life.

So be an active participant in this book and take lots of notes for action items, and ideally take action IMMEDIATELY once you hear something that can help you.

Don't delay, because you know what they say about hesitation, right? He who hesitates *masturbates*.

So don't be the one who hesitates and misses out on the opportunities available for you to move your life forward, right now.

By taking new action and taking new risks, you also build your *confidence,* because when you take action, you can only win. You will either get amazing results, or you will learn, and both are equally valuable.

So take that new *action*, and let's make the rest of your life, the best of your life and become the best you that YOU that you can possibly be.

I salute you, I acknowledge you so much for being such an Action Taker and a Risk Taker, and for beginning this new and powerful journey brother!

Let's begin.

How To Jump-Start Your Success Right Away

"Where there is no vision, the people perish."
-The Bible

K nowing what you really want means becoming SUPER clear on the vision that you want to create in your life.

It means becoming super clear on what you want your life and your relationships with women to look like, overall.

Knowing what you want is about holding a vision in your mind of exactly what you want your future to look like, down to every tiny detail, as much as possible. This is where this whole process really starts.

What kind of relationship do you want to have?

Why do you want that?

What kind of woman do you want?

What traits are most important to you in your ideal woman, physically, mentally, emotionally, and spiritually?

What activities, goals, or experiences do you most want to do, experience, or accomplish with her?

How do you want to FEEL emotionally in you body having all of that in your life?

How do you want to feel about YOURSELF, having accomplished all of that in your life?

It's critical that you first know what you want, because without knowing what you want, you're like a ship without a rudder or a compass. You're like a GPS device that hasn't had any coordinates put into it, so we can't get you anywhere you want to go.

Without knowing what you want, you will end up attracting whatever, even things you DON'T want.

You will get mixed results from women, because you're not going to be able to become the man that your ideal type of woman wants to be with if you don't know *who* your ideal type of woman *is*.

You may think, until this point, that you just need to FIND the right woman to share your life with. When in fact, you need to start BECOMING the man she wants to be with. And if you'd just start with getting clear with what you want and taking that ACTION to get the new support and strategies on your side, you can start creating that new life of your dreams ASAP.

Women also find a man who knows EXACTLY WHAT HE WANTS to be very sexy.

This is because a man who knows what he wants and believes he can have it seems much more CONFIDENT and strong.

It is you stepping into the KING inside of you. A king has a vision, and every time you get even more clear on what you want, you strengthen the king inside to attract your ideal woman to share your throne with.

To get to where you want to go, there are three basic steps:

Number one: You must know where you want to go.

Number two: You must know where you are, right now.

And number three: You must have a clear and specific strategy to get from where you are, now, to where you want to go.

This process starts with getting crystal clear on what you want, deep down in your heart and deep down in your soul, deep down in your balls, and in the fundamental fibers and cells of your being.

So how do you start this process on getting clear on what you want?

Well, to start, I'm a big fan of going inward and then journaling as one of the quickest ways to get clear on what you want. So, I recommend doing this as an exercise:

Begin by sitting down in a quiet location, close your eyes, take a deep breath, and clear your mental slate.

Imagine your mind is like a cluttered table. Imagine swiping the table clean, and everything that was on it is floating up into space or dissolving into the soil, so you have a nice, white, clean slate in front of you.

Next, ask yourself this powerful question and see what might come up for you: When it comes to dating and romantic relationships in your life, if we could wave a magic wand and create ANYTHING you could want to create in your life, what's the most important thing to you and what do you really want deep down in your heart and deep down in your soul?

What do you really want?

Sit with that for a moment, and see what comes up for you.

What does that vision look like?

What are you doing?

What kind of woman are you with?

What does she look like?

What is her smile like?

What is her energy like?

How tall is she?

What's her hair color?

What's her eye color?

What ethnicity is she?

What age is she and what does her body look like?

What does her laugh sound like?

What does her voice sound like?

What does it feel like to cuddle with her and kiss her?

What does her skin feel like?

Start to put yourself in the picture and see what kind of things you are doing together.

Are you walking on the beach together?

Are you just cuddling at home and watching fun TV shows?

Are you having a romantic dinner at a nice restaurant?

Are you traveling the world together, seeing places, like Europe, South America, or Asia?

How much fun are you having together?

Are you having an amazing family together?

Raising kids together?

Are you having amazing sex together?

Are you having great conversations and connecting emotionally?

How attracted are you to this woman?

How much LOVE do you share between the two of you?

See yourself living that ideal life experience and that ideal relationship with her, right now, and start to FEEL that vision emotionally in your body. (This will send that vision directly to your subconscious.)

How does it make you FEEL to have all that in your life, and how do you WANT to feel in your body, having all of that in your life?

How would having all of that in your life and having accomplished that in your life make you feel about *yourself*?

Would you feel so much more confident?

Would you feel so much more love, support, security, bliss, fulfillment, or contentment?

How you want to feel deep down in your body is important, because this gets your subconscious programming aligned towards going for what you want, with nothing held back.

It gets you EXCITED and MOTIVATED again to take new ACTION and to grow and to change and to become the MAN you need to become to create this in your life.

Next, after you have this vision and what it looks like, grab a piece of paper in your journal or on your computer, and write down that full vision in every detail of what you want.

In my 1:1 "Find The Right Woman" Strategy Sessions that I do with my clients, I do a powerful exercise where I help you to get super clear on what you want and what might be stopping you or blocking you from having what you really want.

I've had many men tell me the process by itself made the biggest difference for them in starting to attract their ideal type woman into their life.

After doing this work for over 13+ years, here are just a few examples of things that a lot of men come to me wanting:

→ To Find The Right Woman For You To Share Your Life With & Be Happier ASAP
→ To Have A Loving, Long-Term & Supportive Relationship
→ To Have More Love In Your Life
→ To Meet More Women
→ To Be Much More Confident
→ To Have Even Better Conversations
→ To Be Happy
→ To Have Better Dating Skills
→ To Have The Women That You're Interested In Be Highly Interested In You Also
→ To Talk To Women Better
→ To Be More Social
→ To Have A Loving Family Of Your Own

→ To Be Much More Attractive To Quality Women
→ To Have Quality Women Be Into You
→ To Be Able To Approach Women Easily
→ To Have A Loving Partner
→ To Have A Deep Connection
→ To Take Advantage Of More Opportunities
→ To Enjoy Life More
→ To Feel Complete
→ To Have A Best Friend
→ To Share Life Experiences Together
→ To Travel The World Together
→ To Have More Support In Your Life
→ To Have Great Sex
→ To Have A Girlfriend
→ To Have A Companion
→ To Get Married To An Amazing Woman
→ To Have More Success
→ To Have Better Communication Skills
→ To Be More Comfortable
→ To Have Much More FUN In Your Life
→ To Improve & Grow Together
→ To Have More Self-Esteem
→ To Find Your Soulmate
→ To Be Excited
→ To Have More Passion & Intimacy In Your Life

Clarity is so powerful, because this allows you to create this life you want to have. It all starts with clarity.

My wife and I like to say clarity is King, because it is the starting point for this whole process of what we want to create for you.

The great thing about clarity is you can never get TOO clear. You can always go deeper and deeper. And through life experience, contemplation, thinking, and feeling about it in your heart, you can continuously get clearer on what you want, and you can create that reality for yourself quickly.

So keep going deeper, keep looking for the minor details of what excites you and what revs up your engine, because that EXCITEMENT will help you to make the changes you need to make and getting the right strategies and support on your side to make that a reality.

This conversation also reminds me of one of my amazing clients, Michael L. from San Francisco.

Before Michael met me, he was single and had been struggling with his relationships for several years. He was feeling lonely and frustrated with his dating, since nothing was moving forward or going anywhere romantic for him.

We did a 1:1 "Find The Right Woman" Strategy Session that he signed up for with me, and after getting clear on what he wanted and what the next steps were for him, he became SUPER motivated to make a change and to go for what he wanted, deep down inside.

We started a coaching process of checking in regularly and outlining the personalized strategies and techniques for him, making sure he was consistently taking new right ACTION towards meeting and attracting the quality women he wanted to be with and building his confidence and social skills even more.

He was extremely motivated and committed, and within just a few weeks, he went out to a great social event that I'd recommended to him. And at this event, he was using everything I taught him and what we practiced, and at the event he met a very attractive woman, who he connected with, and they started dating shortly afterwards.

We had another coaching call while he was dating her, and I asked him how things were going, and he told me that things were great, except she was a vegetarian and she didn't drink.

And I said, "Wow, those are some serious red flags," jokingly. And then I asked him how he felt about her, and he said that he felt great and loved his time with her, so I suggested he continued seeing her to see how things might unfold.

And only a few weeks after that call, she invited him to go on a trip to go visit her parents in China. They went and had an amazing time, and I got to see a lot of the great Facebook photos from that. And shortly after they came back from that amazing trip, they moved in together!

A few more months went by, and they are now happily married! Most importantly, Michael feels so much more love, confidence in himself, happiness, and fulfillment in his life that he never thought was possible to have with such a high-quality woman, and he's so proud of himself and the new risks he could take to create the loving relationship of his dreams with her.

And Michael's whole journey started with the 1:1 "Find The Right Woman" Strategy Session we did together, where I helped him to get even more CLEAR on what he wanted, uncovered what was blocking him from having that, and also got clear on the next best steps for him. Clarity is where this whole process starts!

So what's next, and what do I recommend you do with this now, specifically?

Well, the first thing I recommend is doing the exercise I mentioned on getting super clear on what you want and continue to think and get excited about what you want to create in your romantic life with women and dating...

What do you want to create that would get those juices flowing for you?

Feel it in your bones, feel it in your balls, feel it in your cells, and get EXCITED, because that energy will be the rocket fuel to allow you to change and to take the new action steps to get the right support and mentorship on your side and accomplish what you want.

I also highly recommend signing up for a 1:1 "Find The Right Woman" 60 Min Phone Strategy Session with me! This is where we can get on the phone together, just you and me, for about 60 minutes, and I can help you get super clear on what you want, right now, when it comes to women and dating in your life, if ANYTHING were possible for you, and then what things might be *stopping* you or *blocking* you from having what you want.

I can then give you some powerful new strategies, resources, and recommendations to help you to get from where you are, now, to where you want to be ASAP!

And this session with me is normally valued at two hundred and ninety-five dollars. However, as a special gift for purchasing this book, and because I'd like to connect with you and learn even more about what you're dealing with specifically, to make my future books even more valuable to you, you can have this entire session with me as my gift to you on a <u>Full Scholarship</u> for *completely complimentary!*

All you have to do to book this powerful 1:1 session with me is go to my online special website I've set up for this, Right Now at www.HowToFindTheRightWoman.com, and fill out the powerful Breakthrough Blueprint form I have there, and then you'll get sent to my online calendar, where you can select the best day and time that works for you, and we can get things rocking and rolling for you!

I do have very limited spots available for these sessions, I'm not sure how long I'll be offering them, and they will go quickly on a first claimed, first reserved basis, so make sure to claim yours, right now, while you can! (And if it's still available on the special website at www.HowToFindTheRightWoman.com, then you're good to go!)

Awesome man! So hopefully, that can be a great resource for you to get started powerfully on this journey and get the right new strategies and support on your side. I look forward to talking with you more on our 1st powerful 1:1 session together!

And that leads us to our next powerful discussion about commitment, the key to getting the rocket ship off of the ground and staying in orbit, now that we've pointed it in the right direction...

The Secret Sauce Of Attraction

"Desire is the key to motivation, but it's determination and commitment to an unrelenting pursuit of your goal - a commitment to excellence - that will enable you to attain the success you seek."
-Mario Andretti

BRODERICK BOYD

Commitment is that feeling within you, when you are so dedicated to something that you're willing to do WHATEVER IT TAKES to make that vision a reality in your life.

Commitment means you're willing to do whatever it takes, no matter how much energy it takes, no matter how much time it takes, no matter how much money it takes, no matter how much willpower it takes to make that vision come true.

It's like that place where I got in my journey, in the midst of my depression, where I was done, and I said NO MORE and I put my stake into the ground. I got to that place within me, where I was willing to do whatever it took to never ever have to feel that way again.

Having a high level of commitment is critical to finding the right woman to share your life with.

The reason for that is that commitment is that driving force; it is the motivation and it is the rocket fuel that's going to help your rocket ship launch into orbit to having an amazing life you want to have.

Without that commitment and without that rocket fuel driving your ship, it is eventually going to crash.

It's just not going to make it into orbit.

It's going to get almost there, but then it's going to fall back down, and nothing's going to change for you; nothing new is going to happen in your life. You will continue to be stuck, miserable, lonely and wasting time because that commitment just isn't there.

Without that commitment, you will continue to stay home and alone, rather than work on yourself or get a mentor or a coach and new strategies on your side to make this new life into a reality.

So how do you build this high level of commitment?

The first key, like we just talked about last chapter, is you have to know what you want.

You have to know what you want and WHY you want those things, so you can get fully excited, revved up, and MOTIVATED to get off your butt, take action and create that vision.

Why do you want to have this amazing new woman in your life?

What is having the vision you said that you want going to DO for you and PROVIDE for you that's going to make your life so much better on an even deeper level?

What is it going to make possible for you?

What new activities are you going to enjoy together?

What new goals are you going to accomplish in your life?

How much more confident are you going to feel, and what is that new confidence going to make possible for you and your life?

What new doors will that open for you in your life, your mission, and/or your career?

How's it going to make you feel so much more fulfilled and so much more excited to get up every day?

How's this going to improve and affect the lives of the people closest to you, when you're being this man, who has this ideal relationship?

How's it going to inspire your kids if you have them?

What about your future children that you might have if you want them, how will that inspire them and show them what's possible for them also?

How's it going to inspire your friends, your family, your colleagues, and the people around you, seeing that you have an amazing relationship, being happy, and so much more confident in yourself?

How will this new happiness rub off on them and the people that you interact with?

How will you help them to see what's possible, let them see how to be a better version of themselves?

How could you then help to create a more loving world to live in for your woman, your family, yourself, and the people closest to you?

This new awareness, with the answers to these questions, can help to give you this high level of motivation and commitment to make these new big improvements in your life.

Now the other side of building the high commitment level within yourself to achieve this is to get super clear on what's *stopping* you or *blocking* you from having this in your life.

What's really getting in the way and stopping you from having this amazing woman and this amazing relationship in your life?

If you're not sure what's blocking you or stopping you, ask yourself: What blocks, challenges or issues do you notice coming up within YOURSELF or in your interactions with women (especially the ones that you're really interested in) that could be really blocking your or stopping you from what you want?

After doing this work for over 13+ years, here are just some of the big issues, blocks and challenges that I've helped my clients to overcome:

→ Feeling Like You're Wasting Time
→ Fear
→ Fear Of Failure
→ Fear Of Rejection
→ Rejection
→ Low Self-Confidence
→ Low Self-Esteem
→ Loneliness
→ Frustration
→ Depression
→ Sadness
→ Nervousness
→ Poor Social Skills
→ Regret
→ Overthinking
→ Shyness
→ Introvertedness
→ Awkwardness
→ Stress
→ Misery
→ Inadequateness
→ Being Creepy
→ Anger
→ Feeling Resigned
→ Feeling Like A Loser

→ Feeling Inferior
→ Disappointment

To dig even deeper, use some of these other super powerful questions:

What have been your past relationship patterns?

What women were you interested in your past or had a relationship with, and why didn't that go anywhere?

What would you say is the #1 most painful or frustrating thing about where you're at, right now?

How old are you now, and how long have you been single? Why?

Once you've gotten clear on the biggest blocks, challenges, issues and frustrations, we then need to get clear on what those blocks are *costing* you, and what you're *missing out* on because of those blocks, which will move that motivation even higher.

What is it costing you to have these blocks, challenges, issues and frustrations getting in the way, and to not have what you really want?

What is it costing you not to feel that happiness every day and to have the loneliness, fear, anxiety, sadness, frustration, rejection, anger, or depression running your life?

What are you missing out on because of that?

What experiences in your life are you missing out on?

What kind of connection and what kind of great memories are you missing out on in your life, because you're not having this amazing woman and higher levels of confidence in your life?

I love the story of Charles Dickens's "The Christmas Carol", because in that story, Ebenezer Scrooge was this anti-social guy. And as soon as he got visited from the Ghost of Christmas Past and the present, but especially the ghost of the FUTURE, showing him, if things didn't change, where he would end up, things started to really change for him.

The ghost of the future showed him that, if he didn't change his behavior, he would be buried in a remote gravesite at the end of his life, with hardly anyone coming to his funeral.

That's when he got present to the pain in his life and where things were heading, and he finally got FULLY committed, took MASSIVE ACTION, and made a real lasting change in his life.

What will YOUR life be like, 5, 10, or even 25 years down the road if things continue as they have been until this point?

What will be your FATE if nothing changes for you with this, ever?

What does that vision look like for you, potentially dying alone, or experiencing the pain and deep regret, looking back on a wasted life?

What would that misery, disappointment, depression, or loneliness feel like if you made no big change, and you didn't go for what you really want?

If you didn't do EVERYTHING that you possibly could to make what you really wanted into a reality?

Imagine the pain of the regret of missing all those amazing memories you could have had, and all these amazing visions of the life you wanted to have.

Ponder that…

And now turn up the pain of the experience of that event 20X higher.

How would that make you FEEL deep down in your bones if that really were the case?

Because that really is where things are likely heading for you if a big change isn't made here.

And when would NOW be a good time to change this?

Getting present to those visions can give you a huge boost, drive, and MOTIVATION to make these serious new improvements and upgrades, getting the right strategies, mentorship, and support with this area of your life.

This topic also reminds me of one of my amazing clients, Dan M. from Seattle Washington.

Before Dan met me, he was just not having any connections with women, and he was being put into the friend-zone often, and he was feeling really frustrated, angry, and lonely about that.

Then, he found out about me and signed up for a "Find The Right Woman" Strategy Session with me, and in that session, I helped him to get fully clear on what was blocking him, and what it was costing him and what he was missing out on. We built up the motivation to change, and then we got clear on the next steps and what would allow him to move forward with this in his life once-and-for-all.

He got present to that commitment sleeping inside of him, and became a full <u>10 out of 10</u> of commitment!

Shortly after that we did several more phone coaching sessions together, and I helped him to build up his confidence and social skills, I taught him how to approach women without fear, and he started taking massive action and having great conversations with high-quality women, and pretty soon, he enjoyed more romantic connections with beautiful, intelligent women than he knew what to do with!

He had finally stepped up fully and became that man that quality women wanted him to be, and he had the sex life and the love life of his dreams finally, and he's never been happier or more fulfilled with HIMSELF.

So what's next for you with this?

I highly recommend doing that exercise I mentioned about getting clear on what you want, especially WHY you want what you want, and WHY you want that.

Also get clear on what it's going to PROVIDE for you and what's it will make POSSIBLE for you that's going to make your life so much better on an even deeper level.

Then, I highly recommend writing down and getting clear on the biggest challenges, blocks, frustrations, and issues that might be *stopping* you or *blocking* you from having what you want, right now.

What is that costing you, and what are you missing out on because of that?

What will your life be like 5, 10, or 25 years down the road if nothing were ever to change with that?

When would NOW be a great time to make a change?

Write these answers out and journal them and get clear on those items.

Next, I'd also highly recommend again claiming a complimentary 1:1 "Find The Right Woman" Strategy Session with me as well, so we can explore and get clear on what those items are for you, and I can walk you through the process and give you a breakthrough, like my mentor did for me, and help you to get clear on the next new powerful steps, strategies, and resources that will be best for you to move forward quickly. And again, you can claim yours, Right Now, if those sessions are still available on our special members' webpage at www.HowToFindTheRightWoman.com.

Ask yourself, if you're not a full 10 out of 10 commitment, what would it take you to be a full 10 out of 10, or even a full *15* or a *20* out of 10?

Part of that involves deciding that you're no longer going to accept less than the best for yourself, and you're going to RAISE YOUR STANDARDS dramatically for this area of your life.

Decide that you will do *whatever it takes* to make this your reality and have this amazing, loving woman in life to share the rest your life with and be happier ASAP, without loneliness, fear, anxiety, rejection, or wasting any more time!

And now that we have this high level of commitment created inside of you, it's time to stop at nothing and to play full out…

Ways To Make Your Grand Success Inevitable

"You will either step forward into growth, or you will step back into safety."
- Abraham Maslow

So now, hopefully, you've gotten clear on what you want, you've built up your motivation, and you've also gotten clear on what's *blocking* you or *stopping* you from having what you want, and what that's *costing* you, and what you're *missing out* on.

You've also now made the decision to be fully committed, a 20 out of 10, to attracting this amazing woman of your dreams and to doing whatever it takes to become the kind of man you need to be to have this amazing woman in your life ASAP.

Now, it's about stopping at nothing until this becomes your new reality.

It's about doing WHATEVER it takes. It's about not giving up. It's about persisting and making a *decision* that you're going to do whatever it takes, no matter how long it takes, no matter how much energy it takes. To really make this happen.

It's about not stopping at the first sign of rejection or failure, or the first disappointment, or if you get stuck on a plateau where nothing seems to change, or if you get bored or you mess up, or you have negative thoughts.

Whatever happens, it is what it is.

It happens.

Now, the MEANING you put on it will determine if you continue to move forward, or if you get stuck or give up.

So when resistance happens, which is a totally natural and normal part of this process, decide ahead of time to continue to move forward, despite it.

And what's going to happen when you feel that resistance is a stronger part of you, that Kingly part of you, that Mature Masculine part, that part of you will really stand up for you.

It's going to wake up and say a strong <u>NO</u> to that weak, scared, and doubting voice inside of you, and it will say a strong <u>YES</u> to that strong, confident, and committed part of you that holds the vision to have what you really want to have, no matter what.

That stronger Kingly voice and part inside of you will *drive you forward* and allow you to take the new risks and new action steps you need to take to stay COMMITTED and play full out in this process.

And playing full out is about getting out of your comfort zone fully and doing whatever it takes, and giving all your energy and giving your all, putting yourself on the line and being vulnerable, approaching women and going to the right places, where you can meet women and start those conversations.

It's about putting yourself in a position where *you can have success.*

Sure, you might get rejected occasionally, but just like with learning to ride a bicycle or with learning how to walk; you will fall down a few times. But each time you fall down is critical for your learning, and you learn how to become better faster because of it.

So playing full out is about giving it your all, just like athlete at the Olympics; you are giving your all and treating your dating and relationships like a professional.

You're going to practice until you master it, no matter what gets in the way. You're going to keep on keeping on, no matter what challenges, issues, or resistance might come up.

This is so critical to your growth and success, because unless you're willing to stop at nothing, it will be so easy to get thrown off your path and quit and give up. It's going to be so easy.

There will be so many opportunities, when part of you will want to quit.

There's going to be an interaction with a woman that doesn't go well.

There's going to be a rejection that happens or at least your interpretation of a rejection.

There's going to be times when you get bored, times when you doubt yourself, times when you doubt the process or doubt your mentor, times when you're on a plateau.

There's going to be times when you feel like nothing's changed and nothing's happening.

And in those moments, that's when you will remember your commitment, and you will stay on track and keep with the process and continue to practice and practice and practice until you get better at it, and get the results you want to have once and for all.

Meeting, attracting, dating, and keeping a quality woman in your life is a SKILL that anyone can master.

Relationships are a skill.

So treat it like one. Treat it like a professional athlete who's just mastering a new skill.

The best athletes in the world know failure is to be expected and is part of the learning process, which is why they work with a coach and commit to staying committed throughout the process and journey.

There have been so many studies that have been done that show how it's nearly impossible to be fully happy in your life, without having great relationships in your life. Without committing to stop at nothing and playing full out, you're most likely going to end up like so many other mediocre men, who live mediocre lives of comfortable, stuck misery.

You will feel the regret of disappointment in yourself, and the fear, anxiety, doubt, skepticism, cynicism, and frustration will drive your life, and it's not a pretty picture to see.

Don't settle for mediocrity, when greatness is your birthright.

So how do you use this principle?

One way I recommend for you to use this principle is that every time you have resistance coming up, and the Gremlin and inner-saboteur inside tries to talk you out of it, I want you to pull out that list you made of what you want, and look at it and remind yourself of what you're really committed to. Visualize yourself having that new amazing woman in your life in your mind as if you have it already.

See yourself in the picture and feel the emotions you want to feel, having that in your life, and remind yourself of what you're committed to.

Allow it to bring you back and help you to stay committed and to keep on the journey, even in those tough times, no matter what might get in the way.

I also want you to bring out the list of all of the biggest blocks, challenges, issues, and frustrations you're having and what those are costing you and what you're missing out on and remind yourself of that list.

Remind yourself of what your life will be like in the next 5, 10, or 25 years if nothing changes.

Remind yourself of the regret, disappointment, and sadness you will feel if that were the case.

The other key that can help with this is to hire a coach or mentor who can help keep you accountable and keep you on track by checking in with you regularly and guiding you on this purpose.

Working with a coach or mentor is one of the quickest ways to master any new skill in your life, because having someone that keeps you accountable and is in your court with you is the quickest way to make sure you stay committed and persist toward your goal.

They can help you to work through those tough times when the resistance of the fear or the doubt creeps in to help you stay committed to your grand vision of success no matter what.

The other great way to do this is to take new action and take those new risks you know you need to take in the face of the fear or whatever else might come up.

When fear comes up, it's actually a great signal for you to run towards the thing you're most afraid of, because that's going to help you to build your confidence to help you to be playing full out.

Facing your fears and your own resistance is one of the quickest ways to build confidence, and confidence is one of the sexiest things you can have as a man.

So, I highly recommend using that principle and going for it anyways, when resistance comes up, and continuing on the path to play full out and fully express yourself in the way you want to express yourself when you're with quality women or any opportunity where you can approach them or date them.

This conversation also reminds me of a great story of a man named Hernan Cortes.

Hernan Cortes was a Spanish Conquistador, who had a grand vision of one-day conquering Mexico and the Aztec empire.

He had gathered his troops and resources and had set off to Mexico, with his grand vision mapped out and planned thoroughly in his mind.

However, shortly after his troops had finally arrived on the shores of Mexico, there were a lot of mixed emotions and resistance within the troops.

Some were angry, some were frustrated, and some were scared; they didn't have the supplies they needed, and they felt stranded and wanted to go back home to Spain.

Some were becoming potentially mutinous.

Cortes knew what he wanted, however, and he was fully committed to his vision of success.

He wanted to conquer Mexico and go down in the history books, but he knew he wasn't able to do that, unless all his troops were on board and ready to play full out and to stop at nothing to succeed.

So he had a brilliant idea, one night, while his troops were sleeping.

As his troops slept on land, he ordered his personal assistants to sail to the ships that were anchored near the shore and to set the ships on fire.

That next morning, when the troops woke up and looked out at the sea, they saw their ships going up in smoke.

Cortes then addressed them, "Troops, our ships have been burnt to the bottom of the sea. I don't know what happened and we don't know who's responsible, but all we know now is that our only option for survival is to move forward and to conquer the Aztecs!"

His troops then all fell into line with agreement and became highly committed and motivated to succeed, because they now had no other options but to move forward toward their goal, or to perish.

They then began their trek into the jungle, and with only 500 troops Cortes soon conquered the entire Aztec empire of Mexico, which had a population of over 5 million.

So this leads us to one of the biggest secrets to playing full out and stopping at nothing, which is to *burn your ships of retreat.*

This means intentionally cutting out all of your options of retreat or of backing down and making sure you follow through no matter what.

Make it so you have no other option, but to succeed greatly or to perish.

So what are ways that you can do this, specifically?

One way you can do this is to begin by killing all hesitation within yourself. And one of the most powerful ways I recommend doing that in your dating is by doing what's called the 3-second rule.

The 3 second rule is that, as soon as you see a woman you're interested in, you HAVE to start approaching her to say SOMETHING, within 3 seconds of seeing her.

This is great, because you have no chance to overanalyze yourself and get stuck in your own head, and your default then becomes getting into ACTION. Now, by the time you get to her, you will have something to say to her because you HAVE

TO, and the conversation and the practice WILL happen.

A study was done awhile back of the most successful business people in the world. One trait they found they all shared in common was a trait called the Speed of Implementation.

Speed of Implementation means, as soon as they learned something new or something that they needed to do to move them even faster towards the results they wanted, they would do it AS SOON AS POSSIBLE, without thinking or overanalyzing.

They default to ACTION, and that has made them so successful at what they do.

Also, the billionaire entrepreneur Richard Branson has a great phrase, which is "Screw it, just do it!"

And the same principle applies equally to this process and to dating.

Another way you can use this power is if you're in a relationship that's not working. So instead of continuing that relationship and suffering in comfortable misery, using this principle would be to end the relationship NOW, so you're forced to find a new one or at least the real connection, happiness, and love that you're looking for.

Another one of the best ways to do this that I found is to put money down and to hire a coach or join a training program.

The reason this is so powerful, is that by putting down money and having skin in the game, now you HAVE to succeed, and make it work or you will squander your investment!

Your butt is on the line to make the most out of what you've committed to.

PLUS, you now have someone who's going to show up for you to keep you accountable and to MAKE SURE you keep taking the right new action steps to breakthrough to the great new results and the grand vision of success that you have.

No more safety nets!

Often, the reason I see so many single men struggle with this is because things are already good in their life. Things are fine.

I like to call it being "comfortably miserable."

Good is the enemy of great, because when things are "comfortable" or "fine" or "Okay", it gives you no MOTIVATION to want to DO ANYTHING ABOUT IT!

Being comfortable and safe doesn't give them the motivation to do anything different and to change, and that misery can go on for *decades*.

It's also very comfortable and safe to be in an isolated jail cell or in a linen lined coffin, but not ultimately fulfilling to you, I would hope.

To take the island, you have to burn the ships.

No other option but SUCCESS or DEATH!

So what's next?

What I recommend, specifically, is making a list of what you want and what's important to you. Put that list somewhere where you can see it regularly.

Do a visualization exercise on getting aware of what it's costing you, where you're at and what you will miss if you don't change, and what your life will look like 5, 10, or 25 years down the road from now if things don't change.

Then the other great exercise is to put your butt on the line and sign up for a coaching or training program, so you now HAVE to master this area of your life. You will have someone who's there in the vehicle WITH YOU to make sure you get to your destination and help you to work through any inner resistance you may have in the process as well.

It's all about having the right GUIDANCE, STRATEGIES, SUPPORT, and ACTION ITEMS that will move you towards your goal, which leads us nicely into our next powerful chapter that will help you to get those on your side...

The Only Path To Have What You Want Long Term

BRODERICK BOYD

"Things may come to those who wait, but only the things left by those who hustle."
- Abraham Lincoln

Taking new action and taking new risks means doing something you know you need to do that's going to move you closer to your goal.

It means actually doing something.

Not thinking about it, not feeling about it, not planning it, but ACTUALLY DOING something about it.

Taking action is the ONLY WAY real change can happen in your life.

Action is the only way your life can move FORWARD and that something different can come to you.

I love the old saying that, if you change nothing in your life, then nothing changes in your life, and if you want your life to change, then YOU have to change.

I love the quote also from Albert Einstein, which is that "The definition of insanity is doing the same thing over and over again, and expecting a different result."

So we have to do something different if we want our lives to change.

Risk is as also an inherent part of life.

Without risk there is no reward.

Every day, we're taking risks. You could die, you could get struck by lightning, you could get in a car wreck, you could, God forbid, get disease or cancer, and this is all part of the natural process of living.

So we are already facing risk. So the key then is not to AVOID risk, but actually to learn how to MANAGE it, and to get good at taking the RIGHT risks (which a mentor can help you with) and DOING SOMETHING new and facing your fears consistently.

The most successful people in the world will do the things that unsuccessful people are too afraid to do or aren't willing to do.

When you take a risk, there is NO WAY you can lose. Because you win by either taking the action and getting the great results you want to have, or you win by taking the risk and LEARNING what *not* to do and growing your experience, wisdom, and overall attractiveness as a man.

So when you take new action and take new risks in your life, the only outcome you have is to move FORWARD.

There is another great technique from the billionaire entrepreneur Richard Branson, which is that he always says YES. He says yes first, and THEN he figures out how he will make it work. It's the ready, fire, aim principle. You ACT first, and THEN you adjust as you go.

Without action, nothing happens.

Without action, nothing *changes*.

And that's why it's so important to take risks, because when you take risks, you are doing the thing that most people fear doing, which is why most people are comfortably miserable.

The key to succeeding is to do what most people are too afraid to do. Go for it and lean into it. By doing this, you can separate yourself from the crowd, separate yourself from the competition.

You become the one man that the woman will become interested in, because you will stand out from the crowd with your courage and your confidence. And again, confidence is one of the sexiest things you can have as a man.

When you take action, you also get more experience and you get more wisdom, which also improves your overall attractiveness to a quality women. A quality woman will then see you as a man of the world, a wise and experienced man, like a James Bond, Jason Bourne, or Giacomo Casanova.

So take that action and take those risks to increase your attractiveness and improve and change your life to have the ultimate results you want to have and be happier, without doubt, anxiety, or being stuck.

So how can you do this?

The first key is to start with getting clear on what you want. After this, make a list of some of the specific action steps you feel can move you closer to your dreams, and closer to your vision of what you want.

So do that as an exercise, right now, and write a list of what you need to do to move you closer to your dreams.

At the very least, get clear on what the #1 next best action step could be for you to get the new support and strategies on your side.

And that could be as simple as having a conversation, hiring a coach or signing up for a training program, like we mentioned, to get the new powerful support, strategies, and accountability on your side.

It could involve leaving your house and going to a great social event, where you have the opportunity to meet quality women and talk to them.

It could involve practicing your approaches by approaching 5 new quality women and starting a conversation.

It could be building attraction and interest with a woman you've just met.

Or it could be just talking to new strangers and people in your life.

There's so many different things you can do to start to move your life forward, but the key is that you need to take action, because only through ACTION can you learn what's working and what's not working, so you can get better and better results.

Action is also a SKILL that can be learned and a muscle you build.

It becomes a habit, in that the more you do it and be courageous, the more comfortable it will get for you, and you will soon become more comfortable being *uncomfortable* than you used to be with being comfortable.

I like to think of it as similar to leaning back in your chair.

Imagine that you're leaning back in your chair, where the chair is just about to fall over. That's what it feels like to be outside of your comfort zone, where you're always growing.

LIFE happens outside of your comfort zone.

You can only live fully when you're outside of your comfort zone, and growth only happens outside of your comfort zone, so start stretching, stretching, and stretching and taking those new risks you know you need to take.

After that, actually start LIVING your life out of your comfort zone. That's how you make sure that you always keep growing.

This conversation also reminds me of one of my amazing clients, Ruben G. from Phoenix Arizona.

Before we started working together, Ruben was struggling with low confidence, poor social skills, and he had been single for over 5 years, and wasn't having any real romantic connections with women that he was really interested in.

Plus, the only women he was meeting were placing him in the friend-zone, because he wasn't able to generate the attraction, interest, and chemistry he wanted with the women he *was* into.

He was also starting to get very depressed, disappointed, sad, and frustrated going home every day after work to spend by himself, not doing much, and feeling like he was just stuck, angry, and wasting time.

Then he discovered me, and he reached out and signed up for a complimentary 1:1 "Find The Right Woman" Strategy Session with me.

And in the strategy session, we laid out the plan of action of what he needed to do and what the next steps were for him.

He also did even more coaching with me, because he liked that first session so much, and we went deep into the process of helping him to become the ultimate man he needed to be to attract high-quality women, and exactly what he needed to do and what to say step-by-step.

We did some deep processes over the phone, helping him to build his confidence and mastering all of these new powerful social skills and techniques that I taught him.

He was also super committed and motivated, and about 10 days after our initial coaching sessions, he went to this social event that I recommended he go to.

And at the social event, he saw a woman there who was exactly the type of woman he was looking for, at least physically.

And he was using everything we'd practiced and what I had taught him, and he took *action* and took a *risk*, and he went up and started a conversation with her.

And they had a decent conversation! And towards the end of the conversation, he noticed that she was definitely showing some levels of interest and attraction to him, and so he invited her to go on a hike he was planning on that Saturday just outside of the city.

And she said, "Sure, that sounds like fun!" So they exchanged phone numbers, and they met together for the hike on that Saturday.

And on this hiking trip, he was still using everything we practiced and what I had taught him, and they were having great conversations, laughing and connecting, and towards the end of the hike, there was this big waterfall area.

And at the waterfall area, he was noticing that she was definitely showing some strong interest and attraction in him, so he decided again to take *action*, take a *risk*, and he leaned in and kissed her.

And she kissed him back and they made out by the waterfall for a little while, which was great and he was super happy about that.

And then they both went home their separate ways that day. And then about 2-3 days after that, he ended up taking action and texting her and inviting her over to his place for dinner that night, and she said, "Sure, that sounds like fun!" She came over and he cooked her a basic dinner.

And during that evening, he was still using everything we'd practiced and what I taught him, and they were having great conversations and connecting, and toward the end of the night, he noticed again she was definitely showing some strong attraction and interest in him, so he again decided to take *action*, take a *risk,* and he leaned in and kissed her.

And she kissed him back, and she ended up staying over that night, and they hooked up and had sex and the whole thing, which was great.

They continued to see each other about once or twice a week for about 5 or 6 weeks after that. And around the 5-6-week mark, they started realizing that they got along so well, and had such a strong interest and attraction in each other and shared the same goals and interests and activities and love for each other; they decided to have a loving, long-term, committed, and supportive relationship.

And they've been together for about 2 ½ years now, and they're both very happy and doing well in their careers, fully in love with each other, and talking about having a family soon, and he's very ecstatic, happy, and so fulfilled with how this whole journey turned out for him.

So, hopefully, Ruben's story can show you what's possible for you as well, especially with taking those powerful new actions and risks and getting the right support and mentorship on your side and being super committed and motivated to master this.

So some specific action steps I recommend taking is to get very clear on that list of what you want and what things might get in the way, and then what specific action steps you can take to move things to the next level ASAP.

Most likely, one of the new and more powerful action steps for you will be to get the new powerful specific strategies, support, and mentorship on your side, which again, I'd recommend claiming a complimentary 1:1 Strategy Session with me at www.HowToFindTheRightWoman.com to help get started with that.

And if you want to take the island, then burn the boats!

Take that new action, so the weak and scared part of you can no longer overanalyze, debate, dabble, be skeptical, cynical, and stuck, and let the stronger and more courageous Kingly part of you be YES, and make a huge change and get the new accountability, support, and strategies on your side to master yourself, your dating and your relationships fully, once and for all!

And what else could be in the way of that? What is the only thing that tries to stop us? That's right. FEAR! Which is a monster that we can start crushing in our next powerful chapter…

How To Overcome Your Fear Once-And-For-All

"Inaction breeds doubt and fear. Action breeds confidence and courage. If you want to conquer fear, do not sit home and think about it. Go out and get busy."
- Dale Carnegie

Facing your fears head-on means running towards your fears and dancing with your fears in a way you get up close and familiar with them, so they go away and can no longer bother you.

I love the quote from Joseph Campbell (who was an inspiration for the scripts for the Star Wars movies), which you'll probably want to write down, which is "The cave that you fear to enter holds the treasure that you seek."

So what is fear, anyway?

Fear is this primal emotion we have that just wants to keep us safe.

It wants to keep us safe, comfortable, and secure, but not necessarily happy and fulfilled.

We still have this emotion lingering with us from our ancient ancestors, which tries to help us to avoid the saber-tooth tiger, or getting killed by the neighboring tribe; however, it rarely serves us anymore in our modern day-to-day life.

It can become such a strong inhibitor, because it can drive us to live small, safe, secure lives. Just like a prisoner in an isolated chamber or a bird in a cage, or a dead man in a coffin, it can be very comfortable and safe there, but not fulfilling or happy.

So fear will get us to a certain level, but it won't get you to the level you want to be in the long-term.

Start to face your fears, because without doing so, you will be living your life in a box.

You're going to be a shell of your potential.

You're going to be living a life of mediocrity, loneliness, isolation, depression, lack of fulfillment, lack of love and sex, and lack of an amazing life you want to have.

And by facing your fears, you build courage, you build confidence, you build experience, you overcome your fears, you start to ACHIEVE your goals, you ACHIEVE the results you want to have, and you become a better man to live a fully happy and fulfilled life.

You become a more skilled man. You become a wiser man. You become a man others will look up to for inspiration and for courage and for leadership.

You become a leader that people want to follow, and that women become very attracted to and want to date and want to surrender to, because you are this confident man who can guide them and lead them and lead your family to even more happiness and bliss.

Think of it this way. Say you're afraid of something, 10 points of fear, but then when you DO that thing that you're most afraid of, you're automatically awarded 10 points of *confidence*, even if it doesn't go as well as you had hoped.

Most of the fear we have is also simply fear of the unknown.

We become afraid of what we don't know and don't understand.

An old saying about the acronym for F.E.A.R. is False Evidence Appearing Real.

So by running towards your fears and facing your fears, you get up-close-and-personal with your fear and you understand the thing you're most afraid of.

You learn, and you can deal with it and the fear goes away.

It's the same principle with expanding your comfort zone. The more you expand your comfort zone, the more things become comfortable to you, and now you can expand into even bigger and bigger areas of your life.

You become a more powerful man and a more powerful individual.

This is the key to becoming the best and the most attractive man you can be that a high-quality woman will want to be with and want to share her life and be happier with.

So how do you use this principle?

What I recommend is making a list of all the things you're most afraid of in life and in the world.

Get a clear list of your fears, even small things driving you.

What fears are causing you to be stuck and causing you not to be taking action?

Is it a fear of failure?

A fear of rejection?

A fear of looking stupid?

A fear of not being good enough?

A fear of intimacy?

A fear of death?

A fear of success?

After you've gotten clear on your fears, the key is to ask yourself, what are ways that you can think of to face down these fears and eliminate these fears forever?

Some of the ways could just be a small step, like researching that thing you're afraid of. It could be going to experience that thing and looking at it, getting up-close-and-personal to it. Or it could actually be doing the thing you're most afraid of.

It could be EXPERIENCING FULLY that thing that you're most afraid of.

It could be approaching that woman that you're most afraid of talking to.

It could be signing up for that coaching or training program you're afraid of doing or that you're afraid of committed to.

So it depends on what level you're at and how far and fast you want to go, but that's the key to getting clear of your fears.

I love another technique from Will Smith, where he talks about how he hates to be afraid, so he systematically looks for things he's afraid of and does those things, so they no longer bother him, so he can move on to bigger things.

That's the same approach you can take to challenge yourself to become that man of confidence and the best man that you can possibly be.

This conversation reminds me of a great story from the Samurai tradition.

In the Samurai tradition, the Samurai warriors are trained that, when pulling out their swords, they visualize their fear being pulled onto the sword.

And as they are about to go into battle and when they pull out their swords from their scabbards, they see the fear going onto the sword, and then, finally, they hold their sword in front and visualize their fear on the tip of their sword and use that fear to strike down the enemy.

They use that fear to run into battle and face death and the possibility of death, which is often the biggest fear most people have.

And that's what allows them to go into battle and have the confidence and courage they need to succeed on the battlefield.

That's the same approach you can now take as well.

Visualize your fear in front of you and use your fear to compel you into action; use your fear as your motive to go into battle and to take the action you know you need to take.

There's another story that I love about lions and fear.

So lions, when they're hunting a gazelle, often will have the older, slower, and more aged lions wait in the grass, while the younger lions hunt.

While the young lions are hunting the gazelle, they will chase them towards the grass, and as soon as the gazelle gets close to the grass and right before it is about to jump into it, the older lions will jump out of the grass, and they will roar at the gazelle.

Now, the old lions are too old to catch the gazelle, because they're not nimble and fast enough, but the gazelle doesn't know this.

But because the roar from the aged lions scares the gazelle, it will turn around and go backwards and run straight into the claws and the jaws of the younger lions waiting right behind it.

So what does this mean for you?

Well, the gazelles don't realize it, but since the older lions are actually too old to catch them, if they would have just jumped into the roars of the older lions and into their *fear* and into the grass beyond, they could have escaped to their ultimate freedom.

But because they listened to the fear and they gave into it, they hesitated, turned around and were killed.

So, from now on, when you feel that fear coming up inside of you, that fear is not a signal to turn back and retreat to your old way of doing things, but it's actually a signal for you to go straight forward and towards what you want and to jump *through* the fear, because on the other side of the fear is the true freedom, power and everything you want to have in your life that awaits you.

So, some specific techniques that I recommend for using this principle is to make the list of the things you're most afraid of and to then write down ways you can overcome those fears. Also, continue to work with your mentor or your coach and let them guide you on which fears to face and the best ways to overcome them, once and for all.

Often, having someone guide you along the path is one of the quickest ways to help you overcome those things that were actually very easy to overcome.

The other thing is to take action and to look for those things you're afraid of and go for it and face it.

It's like a muscle you work, just like leaning back in the chair, and it gets easier the more you do it.

So think of some fears today you can face down, especially related to your own personal growth or to women, whether it's getting the right support on your side, taking the leap and hiring a coach, or leaving your house and starting a conversation with an attractive high-quality woman that you're very interested in.

Face those fears you have RIGHT NOW and do something that's new and different to you, because *that's* the only way to build that CONFIDENCE that will ultimately bring the high-quality woman you want to have into your life.

Now, what else can add to these fears and even AMPLIFY them? Those are your negative limiting beliefs, which will lead us into our next powerful chapter to stomp those out as well...

How To Create The Right Mindset For Rapid Attraction

"Whether you think you can or you think you can't,
you're right."
- Henry Ford

Beliefs drive us. They drive every emotion we feel, and every action we take.

The recipe is that your thoughts create your beliefs, which create your emotions, which create your actions, which create your habits, which create your destiny.

Beliefs can be formed and can stay with you from your earliest childhood; they can often come from your parents, well-meaning friends, society, government, religion, TV, the media etc.

Beliefs are also similar to weeds and plants that grow in the garden of your mind, where they will continue to grow the more you "water" them, and you "water" your beliefs with your thoughts.

If you believe you don't deserve to have great success with women and relationships, that belief is most likely going to cause you to feel low confidence, which will cause you not to go out or not to approach a quality woman you're interested in.

However, if you believe that you deserve to have an amazing relationship with an amazing woman in your life deep down, THAT belief will cause you to take that new ACTION to get the right support, strategies, and mentorship on your side to talk to high-quality women confidently and have a great relationship with an amazing woman.

You can now see how our beliefs affect everything that can happen to us and our life.

And what do I mean by *reframing* beliefs?

Reframing beliefs is identifying an old belief that no longer serves you and *changing* that belief into a positive and more empowering belief that's going to allow you to change your life to be more confident and to move forward in a positive direction to create the life you want to have.

And beliefs drive EVERYTHING.

I've seen a lot of negative beliefs that come up, especially in single men, that hold them back, such as the belief that they're not good-looking enough, or they're not tall enough, or they're not the right age, or they don't have enough money, or they're not in the right career or financial situation, or they're not good enough in bed, or they don't have a big enough penis, or that they're simply not ready yet.

And these negative, disempowering, and limiting beliefs cause men to live limited disempowering lives, and it causes them to feel low self-confidence about themselves, to not be taking any new actions or new risks and to be stuck and miserable for DECADES.

They feel bad about themselves, they feel bad about their lives, they feel like they have no chance, their confidence is just shot and gone, and they go nowhere with women they're interested in. It becomes a downward spiral.

They become unattractive to women, simply BECAUSE of their beliefs and BECAUSE they're not taking any of those risks they know they need to take to reverse that.

You are in exactly the right place you need to be to have an amazing woman in your life, right now.

You're also the right age you need to be to have your amazing woman in your life.

You're exactly the right height you need to be.

You have exactly the right financial situation you need to have. (It's never about resources anyways; it's about RESOURCEFULNESS.)

You need not have ANY of those things to have the woman you want to have in your life.

Women, throughout time, have been attracted to men long-term, primarily, because of a man's CONFIDENCE, his personality, and his skills.

Those are the things that women will choose over and over again.

This is great, because these are all things you can change as a man and improve by getting the right mentorship, support, and new strategies on your side.

I see this all of the time in the over 13+ years that I've been doing this work; quality women will consistently pick a man who doesn't have the looks, height, finances, age, etc., but who has an amazing personality, confidence, and social skills.

And the reverse is also true; a man can have the looks, the height, the ideal age, etc., and yet, if his personality, confidence, or skills are lacking, the woman will not be attracted to him long-term and will leave him to be with a guy with those inner traits.

That is why your beliefs are so important, because unless you address these beliefs, you will continue to lead a disempowered life, you will not have what you want, you will not go for what you want, and you will not be as attractive a man as you could be.

So by re-framing your old beliefs, you can have the possibility of attracting an amazing woman you can have a loving long-term relationship with, but if you continue to believe in those negative beliefs about yourself, about life, about women, and about the world, it will cause you to continue being lonely and potentially single and unhappy the rest your life.

So how do you start to reframe old beliefs?

The first thing I recommend is to get out a piece of paper or a journal and write one line down the middle of the paper.

Next, on the left side of this line, list all of the negative beliefs you have about yourself, or about women, or about the world, or that you *used* to have about yourself, women, or the world.

These can be old beliefs, such as: "I don't know if I'm not ready yet", or "I'm not good-looking enough", or "I don't have enough money", or "It's not the right time yet", or "I don't have enough time", or "I can't seem to find the right woman", or "There's no good women in my area", or "Women don't like guys like me", or "Women don't like guys of my ethnicity", or "All the women I'm interested in aren't interested in or attracted to me", or "I'm an introvert", or "I'm not famous enough", or "I don't have a good enough body", or whatever those negative limiting beliefs might be.

List them all and get them on paper, because awareness is the first step to changing anything in your life.

Now, on the other side, we're going to reframe each of these old negative beliefs.

And we'll do that by taking all of the old beliefs from the left side, and on the right side, we'll write the positive empowering OPPOSITE of those old negative beliefs.

So if the old belief was "I'm not good-looking enough", your new belief becomes, *"I'm a good-looking guy"*. Or *"My confidence, personality, and skills are the sexiest things to high-quality women."*

If your old belief was "I am not ready yet." Your new belief becomes, *"I am ready, Right Now!"*

If your old belief was "I'm too old." Or "I'm too young." Then your new belief becomes, *"I'm exactly the right age I need to be to have everything that I want!"*

If your old belief was "I'm not confident." Your new belief becomes, *"I'm extremely confident and certain!"*

If your old belief was "Women don't like me because of my ethnicity." Your new belief becomes *"My ethnicity is the sexiest thing about me!"*

If your old belief was "There are no good women out there." Your new belief becomes *"There are TONS of amazing women in my area!"*

If your old belief was that you don't have enough money, your new belief becomes *"I already have EVERYTHING that I need to start creating the amazing life what I want to have!"* or *"It's never about the resources; it's about my resourcefulness!"*

If your old belief was "I can't make this happen for me." Your new belief becomes *"With the right support and mentorship on my side, I can do ANYTHING!"*

Etc.

Now, the other way to use this power is that, whenever you notice yourself having a negative thought or having a negative emotion during the day, look back and discover the thought you just had that gave you that negative emotion.

Once you have identified the thought or belief that gave you that negative emotion, you can start to reframe and replace it with a new and more empowering belief, so you can take that new and more powerful ACTION to have a new and more empowering LIFE!

The other way you can use this power is to write down your new more empowering beliefs on a piece of paper and read them out loud at least once every morning, or whenever you have a negative thought come up that may hold you back during the day.

Repetition and taking massive action is the mother of all skill, so the more you do it, the easier it will get, and you'll get the right support, mentorship, and new strategies on your side to back up and support these new beliefs and this new life you want to have.

This conversation also reminds me of a good story that can help to explain the power of this.

So, there once was a psychologist who studied happiness and who was lecturing around the country. And he had come to adopt the philosophy that people who had more sex were far happier and more confident people.

And so he was doing a talk one night in an auditorium full of people. To demonstrate his point, he asked everyone in the audience who were having sex 3 times a week or more to stand up.

And the people who stood up all looked very happy and confident.

Then he asked them to sit down, and he asked everyone who was having sex less than once a week to stand up.

And they all stood up, and the people who stood up who were having less sex, did not appear as happy or confident as the other group.

Then he said, see, that proves my point!

In the back of the room however, a man was still standing who looked very happy and confident. And the speaker called on him and asked him, "Sir, how long has it been since you last had sex?"

And the man spoke up to him and said "Well, I actually haven't had sex for over a year now... *But tonight's the night!"*

The man who said this, although he had not had sex for over a year, could MANUFACTURE the confidence and the happiness inside of himself, in that moment, because of the BELIEF that the sex-cess that he wanted was COMING TO HIM!

That belief and energy caused by that is very attractive to women, and the man in the story created that confidence in himself, simply *because* of his belief he could have what he wanted to have, that he deserved it, and that it was coming to him soon.

So what are specific ways I recommend using this power?

Well, again, I highly recommend doing the exercise where you list your top limiting negative beliefs you might have about yourself, the world, dating, relationships, or women on the left side of a piece of paper, and then on the right side, write your new and more empowering positive opposite beliefs you will now start adopting.

Repeat these new thoughts and beliefs to yourself frequently by writing them out on a paper you keep with you, reciting them in the mirror every morning, journal about them, visualize them, and start to believe and FEEL these new beliefs; find images that represent them to you and post them in your room or do whatever it takes to make them a new reality for yourself.

No belief we have is "true" per-se anyways, and it doesn't even matter if that belief is factually "true."

The only thing that matters now is: Does this belief serve you and help to move you forward? And the answer to that will help you to identify which beliefs to adopt and which to replace.

We already have these beliefs and thoughts that we're thinking every day. The question is are your thoughts EMPOWERING you, or are they DISEMPOWERING you? Are they moving you forward or holding you back? NOW is the time to take control of your beliefs, to become conscious of them and to start CHANGING YOUR LIFE!

The other benefit of repeating these new and more empowering positive beliefs to yourself is that by doing so, you will activate a particular part of your brain, called "the reticular activator system", and as soon as you think that thought, that part of your brain will look for evidence of that belief to back it up for you and help you in your journey.

This is the same mechanism inside of you, where, for example, after you buy a certain car, suddenly, you now see this same car

EVERYWHERE, because you're now focused on it, and that part of your brain is alerting you to it.

I recommend that you also start to notice your thoughts and take action whenever you notice your thoughts going to a negative place.

I feel I have a specialty and expertise in identifying negative limiting beliefs and hidden fears in my clients, since I've been doing this work with thousands of men all over the planet, and again, I'd love to help support you in identifying what yours might be in our complimentary 1:1 "Find The Right Woman" Strategy Session. Let's get this scheduled for you, Right Now, if you haven't already, because until those old beliefs are brought into awareness and changed, you will continue to live a life of loneliness, frustration, indecision, low-confidence, and inaction.

But when you drop these old hidden beliefs and replace them with new and far more *empowering* beliefs, you'll build a life of high confidence, amazing self-esteem, happiness, and empowerment, which will allow you to take the new ACTION you need to take with the new powerful strategies to attract that amazing, sexy, and loving woman into your life ASAP, without losing any more time!

And that leads us nicely into the power and necessity of having ongoing support in your journey towards the success you want to have…

The Best Strategies To Boost Your Results

"You can't solve a problem with the same level of thinking that created it."
-Albert Einstein

Getting new support, mentorship, and strategies on your side are some of the biggest keys you're going to need to make a big difference with this area of your life.

And support means having someone on your team who is there for you, and who can guide you and identify, specifically, what you're doing right and what you could do better as you go along this path step-by-step.

It's also one of the quickest ways to master any new area of your life.

I've seen a lot of men, who lead very mediocre lives and struggle with asking for help and receiving help, and that's one reason they are so stuck, lonely, isolated, depressed, and living in misery.

You wouldn't try to perform surgery on yourself, would you? That's the equivalent of what most guys are doing when they think they can "figure it out themselves" and do it by themselves.

But what is that costing them? Wasted time. Reinventing the wheel. Spinning their wheels and being stuck even longer. Old patterns and habits are also harder to change the longer they go on.

The problem with that approach is that you don't know what you don't know, and it almost always takes an expert outside of you to identify, specifically, what is going on within you and show you what you didn't realize that you didn't realize. (And most things that will make the biggest difference for you with this are things you didn't know that you didn't know).

A big part of this is about the minds you surround yourself with and from whom you're getting your advice.

It's so important to make sure you're getting your advice from the right sources.

If you're getting advice from people who are also single and have no quality or loving long-term relationship that you want to have, then all they can help you do is continue to be single and alone and to have what they've created.

There's an old saying from the classical personal development guru Jim Rohn, which is that "You tend to become like the 5 people that you spend the most time around." You have the same levels of relationship success, career success, financial success, health success etc.

So, it's VERY important who you get your advice from and spend your time around and learn from people who have the loving relationship you want, and who aren't also single, alone, and struggling.

Getting quality mentorship and having the right support and mentorship on your side is one of the fastest ways to master any new area of your life, because support and mentorship keeps you accountable to make sure you're taking the right action and make sure you're staying on the right course. It's literally the shortcut, through the shortcut.

The beauty of getting coaching is that it is specifically customized and personalized just for you, which makes it so much faster, more powerful, more efficient, and more effective as opposed to just reading a book or inhaling more data online.

In this day and age, where things are developing and moving so quickly, generalized information just doesn't cut it. We need SPECIFIC information that's PERSONALIZED FOR US and for our current situation, so you know exactly what the next step is for you.

This is also important, because some advice that might work for one person could be actually the OPPOSITE advice that would work the best for you, and working with a quality mentor and getting quality support is the best way to identify that and know for sure.

A wallflower will have a far different path than a Don Perignon, although both will need that personalized support to get to the next level.

Like I said before, it's important to surround yourself with people lifting you up, because it's like what they call the "crab in the bucket" syndrome.

And the "crab it the bucket" syndrome is that, when you put a bunch of crabs in a bucket, you need not put a lid on the bucket or worry about them crawling out, because as soon as one crab starts to climb out the bucket, the rest of the crabs will pull him down, because they'll try to get out as well.

So that explains the old saying that misery loves company.

Be careful who you hang out with and make sure they have what you want, because as soon as you become successful, they will subconsciously try to pull you back down to their level.

Instead of that, when you have a mentor who has what you want and who has helped many others to get what they have, it's like they are sending a ladder down to you that you can climb out and go to the next level, and they can show you exactly what next step to take to get to where you want to go fast.

They will help you along the way, when the fears and insecurities come up, so they can help you work through them and help you get where you want to be ASAP.

There is a gap from where you are now to where you want to be, and that gap is called your potential. Working with a mentor is the bridge. It is the ladder that will get you from where you are now to where you want to be the quickest, so getting new mentorship and support on your side is critical to success.

So how do I recommend doing this?

The first key is to get clear on what you want and why you want that. The next key is to find someone with what you want, who has helped others to have that as well, and to hire them as your coach.

Hire someone who can show you the path because it's been done before, so why waste more years trying to reinvent the wheel?

Let them become your Yoda.

Choose a mentor, whose story inspires you, who started in a similar place you are in, with what you want to have now, who has helped many others achieve the same thing, and who you can relate to.

This topic reminds me of one of my favorite stories, which is the story of The Count of Monte Cristo.

And the story of the Count of Monte Cristo starts with a young French sailor, named Edmond Dantes.

Edmond had gotten into a relationship with a young and beautiful woman before leaving for a long trip at sea. When he arrived back home, not only was he reunited with his love, but he was fortunate and excited to discover he had received a promotion and would be made Captain of the ship.

However, his best friend, Fernand Mondego, was very jealous of him and wanted to sabotage his success with his career and with his relationship.

So Fernand Mondego shared with the local authorities he had seen a letter pass between the hands of Edmond Dantes and Napoleon Bonaparte when they had an emergency landing on the island of Elba.

Because of this news, Edmond Dantes was taken into the authorities and questioned and found guilty of treason.

He was then sent to the island of Chateau D'If to spend his life in prison.

In this prison, he was placed in a dark dungeon, where he was tortured and isolated.

After being in prison for a few years, he became so depressed that he tried to kill himself, unsuccessfully.

One day, however, he noticed a ticking noise underneath the cell room floor, and an old man dug up from the floor.

Edmond was very scared at first, but he then realized this old man was his next-door cellmate, who had been digging for months, thinking he was ending up on the other side of the prison to escape, but ended up in his neighbor's cell instead.

They got to know each other, and they soon hatched a plan to dig their way to freedom together.

This old man (who used to be a captain in the army) also soon became his mentor.

While they were working towards their escape, the old man taught Edmond all of the ways of being a man, including politics, mathematics, strategy, women, warfare, fighting, and human psychology.

They discussed what had happened, and why Edmond had been betrayed by his best friend, Fernand, and what he could have done differently and what he could do after they escaped from the prison.

The old man also gave him something very special.

That gift he gave Edmond was a map that showed him how to get to a secret treasure buried on a remote island.

So they were digging for months together, and then one day, the tunnel they were digging unfortunately collapsed on top of them, and the old man was killed.

Edmond then pulled the old man's body into his jail cell, and the prison wards found the old man's dead body there.

The prison wards got a body bag to put the deceased old man in and wrapped him up and left him there, until they were ready to discard the old man's body.

While they had left, Edmond snuck into the old man's jail cell and pulled the old man out of the body bag, put the old man's body into the tunnel they had dug, and put himself into the bag instead.

Then, when the jail workers took the body bag with Edmond inside and threw it off the cliff and into the ocean, Edmond was thrown into the ocean instead, and he was free.

After his escape, Edmond then used the map he was given by his mentor, and he found the buried treasure. He then became extremely wealthy, and he became The Count of Monte Cristo.

He then began a process of systematically getting revenge on Fernand Mondego and the others who had betrayed him and he won back his woman.

He then solidified his kingdom with his beautiful woman by his side, and together, they lived happily ever after.

This story inspires me, because it shows you the power of what it means to have a mentor by your side, helping you to find the "treasure" in your journey and learning the skills and taking the action and the new risks to create that beautiful life of your dreams.

So what's next?

I recommend, specifically, to start by getting even more clear on what you want and then to ask yourself, who has what you want and who can help you on this journey?

Who has a loving long-term relationship and success with women and dating that you'd like to have, and who has helped other single men to create that as well?

Next, take action and hire them as your coach and surround yourself with people, who have what you want who can lift you up.

Again, if you'd like to explore and see what it's like to work with a mentor and how quickly I can help you to get started with this process, I would love to support you and your journey. So, if you'd like to claim your free sample of a free session and see what it's like to work with me, again, go to our special website link, Right Now, at www.HowToFindTheRightWoman.com and book the best day and time that works for you!

I'd love to explore and learn more about what you're struggling with, specifically, to help make these future books even more valuable to you as well and start jump-start your life to the next level, ASAP!

Which nicely leads us into our last powerful secret to ignite your rocket ship, which is to make a new key DECISION for yourself and to go for the life of your dreams and do whatever it takes to succeed quickly...

The #1 Most Powerful Decision That You Need To Make

BRODERICK BOYD

"Your life changes the moment you make a new, congruent, and committed decision."
-Tony Robbins

Now that we've gone through this journey together, it's now time for you to make a powerful decision.

This is the time for you to decide if you will continue to live your life as it has been up until this point, or if you will decide to do something different.

If you will decide to raise your STANDARDS and have something SO MUCH better in your life, something you've always wanted to have, something that's not just good, but that is GREAT and OUTSTANDING.

If you're not willing to take the risk and take the massive action to go for what you want, then nothing can change or get better for you.

So now is the time to make that decision.

Very successful people decide quickly, and I recommend you practice this, right now.

Look within yourself and ask, *"When will NOW be a good time to change?"*

"When will NOW be the time to go for it and make this a life journey you want to have?"

"When will NOW be a good time to do something completely different?"

And make that decision right now.

Either a yes or no.

Write your decision on the side of this book or on a piece of paper; write a yes if you're really going to go for what you really want, and if you're willing to do whatever it takes to get the right support and strategies on your side and make this happen no matter what, or write a no if you will continue with the status quo and the way your life has been until this point.

Once you've made that decision, I want you to write one powerful massive action step that you will take.

What's that next most logical powerful step for you to get the new support and strategies on your side and get into ACTION and accountability with this ASAP?

Once you've written that down, DO that thing. Take action and do that action step RIGHT NOW and start the journey to your new life destiny NOW.

Making a decision means, literally, to cut off the other options.

It's just like I said earlier. To take the island, you have to burn the ships of retreat. Burn all of the safety nets.

Make a decision.

Don't allow yourself to continue down a path that hasn't been fully satisfying to you.

Decide to do something different and radical for you. Do something you have never done. Don't settle for less anymore and go for what you REALLY want to have in your life.

Take those new actions and those new risks, because without that, you will continue to miss all of the amazing opportunities and memories you could have in your life. It will cost you the great fulfillment and completeness of living your full life purpose, and you will continue to be stuck, lonely, sad, rejected, anxious, fearful, and feeling like you're a loser and letting even more time slip past you.

So make that decision now to make that change, because without it, nothing's going to happen, and with it, EVERYTHING can happen and everything good can come to you.

To help with this, a powerful exercise you can do is to write down everything that you want and then to write what's stopping you from having what you want. Then write what that's costing you and what you're missing out on.

Finally, write down one specific next action step you will take to get the right support and mentorship on your side and to take Massive Action towards going for what you want.

Face your fears head on, because risk taking is what's going to allow you to change your life.

This conversation also reminds me of one of my last favorite stories for this book.

So, there once was a tiger cub that had been abandoned by his mother, because his mother had been killed in a fire.

And this tiger cub was lost and scared, wandering about the jungle, not sure what to do, and he soon wandered into a wide-open grassy field.

And in this grassy field, he found a flock of sheep.

And he didn't know what else to do, so he fell in line and he became one of the sheep.

He ate the grass with the sheep, and he even started baa-ing like the other sheep, and for all intents and purposes, he actually BECAME a sheep.

Years went by, as he continued to live this way, living this very mediocre and comfortably miserable life, eating grass he didn't even enjoy.

Then, one day, an older adult tiger happened upon this grassy field.

The adult tiger saw this flock of the sheep, and he started to hunt them.

As he was just upon the sheep, he started running towards them, and the sheep ran and scattered. And while he was chasing the sheep, he saw this young tiger amongst the sheep, running and screaming as well.

The adult tiger was very surprised by this, and ran after the younger tiger, specifically, and soon caught up to the younger tiger and pinned him down on the grass.

The younger tiger was kicking and screaming, and soon, the older adult tiger shouted at him:

"WHAT ARE YOU DOING!?"

And the younger tiger was confused, because he could understand the words of the older tiger, and the adult tiger said:

"YOU ARE NOT A SHEEP. YOU ARE A TIGER!!!"

And the young tiger was resistant and confused and tried to get away, so the adult tiger commanded, "Here, come with me, and I'll prove it to you."

And he pulled the younger tiger over to the river and said, "Here, look!" and showed him the reflection of who he really was.

And the young tiger was shocked.

But he finally got it.

He was not a sheep; he was a Tiger.

HE WAS A F%#@ING TIGER!

After he finally realized this and his full potential, from that day on, he started living like the strong and powerful tiger he was.

And he was mentored by the older tiger, and soon, he rose through the ranks and became the most powerful tiger in the jungle, ruling his tribe, and marrying a beautiful tigress and having many beautiful cubs together, and living happily ever after.

So the moral of the story is that you are not a sheep.

<u>YOU. ARE. A. F%#@ING TIGER!</u>

So stop PRETENDING to be a f%#$ing sheep!

Often, we are taught by our parents, society, our well-meaning friend, school, religion, etc. to be so much less than what we are.

Now is the time to change that.

Now is the time to own your full POWER as a man and STEP IT UP!

Let's start this journey NOW; there's no more pretending.

There's no more faking it.

There's no more pretending things are good when there's something so much greater waiting inside of you for you to make that decision NOW and start to take that new action to start creating this new life of your dreams, starting today.

Raise your standards of what you're willing to accept!

So we're coming near the end here of our journey, for now.

But this is actually just the beginning.

And the beginning is you lighting the fuse of your new self and your new rocket ship that is your life to shoot off into orbit.

Sign up for a new and different life.

So what are these next steps for you?

What are you going to do now to get the right support your side, get the right mentorship, take massive action, face your fears, play full out, stay committed, and do whatever it takes to make this a new reality for yourself, no matter what?

Now is the time to take this new action!

Everything we've outlined in this book, do the exercises and recommendations. Start this process, take those risks, and get on the journey of upgrading yourself and creating your new life.

Again, I'd love to support you on this journey, and if you've resonated with anything in this book, and you know you're committed to doing whatever it takes to get that new support and strategies on your side and take action and make this happen for yourself, claim your complimentary 1:1 "Find The Right Woman" Strategy Session with me Right Now at www.HowToFindTheRightWoman.com.

You can also reach us anytime by email at Brody@HowToFindTheRightWoman.com.

I'd love to hear all of your thoughts and questions, it's my honor to accompany you on this new development and the beginning of a massive upgrade of your entire life, and I look forward to supporting you to get from where you are now to where you want to be ASAP, fully forming a plan of action and a strategy. Let's make the rest of your life the best of your life, once-and-for-all!

I salute you, I acknowledge you for being such a highly committed Action & Risk Taker stepping out of your comfort zone, and let's do this man!

Much love to you brother! ♥

To your commitment to finding lasting love in your life quickly, without fear,

-Brody

~Dreams Can Come True~

"If you wait, all that happens is that you get older."
- Mario Andretti

ABOUT THE AUTHOR

Broderick (Brody) Boyd struggled for YEARS with fear, low confidence, rejection and was on the verge of suicide before he finally broke through, hired a dating coach, had great success with women & dating and met his beautiful, loving and supportive wife Antia! He has now been helping single men all over the world to find the right woman to share their life with & be happier ASAP without loneliness, frustration or wasting any more time for over 13+ years. He has a degree in communications and interpersonal relationships, is a published author, has spoken on stages and radio shows all over the US, and for over a decade studied everything that he could get his hands on in the areas of women, dating & building great confidence & social skills quickly without fear.

Printed in Great Britain
by Amazon